James W.

Finding
Bethlehem
in the Midst of Bedlam

Mike Poteet

An Advent Study for Youth

Table of Contents

Introduction

Are You Ready for Christmas?

At some point in our lives Christmas goes from being a holiday that we eagerly anticipate to a holiday that we hope doesn't arrive before we're ready for it. Small children look forward to Christmas, counting down every moment, starting with the moment that the dishes are put away following Thanksgiving dinner. By the time Christmas Eve arrives, they're so excited that they can't sleep.

But as people get older, many wish that time would slow down during the month of December so that they'll be able to complete everything on their to-do lists. They have to finish their shopping, prepare food for Christmas parties and gatherings, clean the house for guests, and manage a busy schedule of seasonal events. Many adults also cannot go to sleep on Christmas Eve. But it's not because they can't wait to wake up on Christmas morning and see the gifts under the tree. It's because they have too much to do.

So where do youth fit into all this Christmas busyness? You may not have the hosting responsibilities, or even the lengthy shopping lists, that your parents have. But you are well past the age where you can spend December writing letters to Santa and snooping for gifts. If you attend a school that ends its fall semester shortly before Christmas, you probably have finals to study for or semester projects to finish. If you're involved in music or drama, you may have seasonal concerts or shows to rehearse. If you play sports, you might have to manage time constraints between game and practice schedules and family gatherings. If you have a boyfriend or girlfriend, you may feel a lot of pressure to find the perfect gift. Sometimes this season in which we prepare our hearts and lives for all the ways in which Christ enters our world feels like bedlam.

The word *bedlam,* as you will learn in the first session of this study, is actually related to the name of the city in which Jesus was born on the first Christmas: Bethlehem.

As we approach Christmas, we're supposed to turn our eyes toward Bethlehem. We're supposed to remember how God became human in the form of an infant and in the most humble of circumstances. But it's hard to keep our eyes trained on Bethlehem when we're surrounded by bedlam.

FINDING BETHLEHEM IN THE MIDST OF BEDLAM is about focusing on the birth of the Messiah, noticing the ways Christ continues to come into our lives, and remembering Christ's promised return even amid all the chaos and busyness of the season.

Focusing attention on what God is doing even when life is crazy was as relevant a concept in biblical times as it is for us today. Jesus' mother Mary, after an unexpected pregnancy and enduring a long and uncomfortable journey from Nazareth to Bethlehem, had to give birth in someone else's stable. The shepherds who visited Jesus shortly after his birth were in a dangerous and unforgiving profession, and their evening had been interrupted by a frightening yet heavenly music-and-light display. John the Baptist's ministry of repentance drew the ire of those in power. And the apostle Paul had to explain the good news of God's Son being "born through a woman" to a church that couldn't seem to grasp the concept of God's grace.

This study looks at these stories of biblical bedlam and explores what these Scriptures can teach us about how to attune ourselves to Jesus during a time of year when so many other things demand our time, energy, and attention.

How to Use This Leader Guide

Though this resource is for youth, the book itself is set up like an adult Bible study. Everyone, whether leader or participant, has the same book and literally is on the same page.

FINDING BETHLEHEM IN THE MIDST OF BEDLAM includes five sessions, one for each Sunday of Advent and one for Christmas Sunday. In this book, each session begins with a key Scripture and an article relating the biblical account of Jesus' birth to the seasonal bedlam that we experience today. The Scripture and article are followed by a session plan, which includes three parts:

❖ *Light the Advent Candles*: Each session begins with an opening liturgy that includes lighting Advent candles and a responsive reading that incorporates several key Scriptures.

❖ *Hear God's Word*: Following the candle lighting, participants read and reflect on the key Scripture and weekly article. Your group can read the weekly article during their time together, or participants can read it in advance.

❖ *Respond to God's Word*: Every session includes a variety of learning activities and discussion starters that explore ways in which Christians can apply each week's lesson. Your group can choose the options that are best suited to your size and setting and participants' learning styles.

Six daily devotional readings accompany each session. Spend time each day during the Advent and Christmas seasons reading Scripture and reflecting on how you can stay focused on Christ, even in the midst of bedlam.

WEEK ONE

Bedlam

Luke 2:8-14

Nearby shepherds were living in the fields, guarding their sheep at night. The Lord's angel stood before them, the Lord's glory shone around them, and they were terrified. The angel said, "Don't be afraid! Look! I bring good news to you—wonderful, joyous news for all people. Your savior is born today in David's city. He is Christ the Lord. This is a sign for you: you will find a newborn baby wrapped snugly and lying in a manger." Suddenly a great assembly of the heavenly forces was with the angel praising God. They said, "Glory to God in heaven, and on earth peace among those whom he favors."

A New Word for Madness

bed • lam *n.* a state of confusion or commotion

"In that place be found many men that be
fallen out of their wit."[1]

That's how William Gregory, a mid-fifteenth century mayor of
London, described the institution known today as Bethlem Royal Hospital.
One of the first hospitals to specialize in treating people with mental
illness, Bethlem Hospital is today a modern research and treatment
facility. In past centuries, however, its patients endured neglect and abuse,
cruel confinements, and rough restraints. People who passed by its gated
courtyard could hear "the cryings, screechings, roarings, brawlings,
shaking of chains, swearings, frettings, chafings"[2] of those inside.

The place had been named, at its founding, after Bethlehem—the
"little town" where Jesus was born, lying so still in dreamless sleep (as
Christmas carols tell us). But, because these sounds of suffering so came
to define it, the hospital's original name gave way to another name, a word
meaning, according to most dictionaries, "a state of uproar and confusion."
That word? You guessed it: *bedlam*.

Does Christmas Drive You Crazy?

I don't know how you experience the holiday season, but more than
one December has found me groaning, "Christmas is driving me crazy!"
Why? The incessant advertising, for starters. This year I saw my first TV
commercial starring Santa in September—a new record. And all those
ads make me think about the shopping I'll be doing and the presents
I'll be buying. Then there's decorating the tree and decking the halls,
along with extra church commitments and neighborhood parties. And the
soundtrack for all this busyness? Those radio stations that insist on playing
holiday music 24-7 from Thanksgiving through December 25. Now, I like
Christmas music, but I only want to hear so many renditions of "Jingle
Bell Rock!"

I hope your experience of Christmas isn't a crazy one. After all,
Christmas means time off from school, right? No homework for a week or

two. And the adults in your family are probably the ones handling most of the holiday logistics. As a teen I never found the Christmas season crazy. It was a time for sleeping in, staying up late, plenty of free time, and lots of good food.

Of course, for many people, Christmas doesn't bring a break from life's problems and pressures. The season's emphasis on giving and receiving gifts can strain the nerves of families scraping by on tight budgets as parents look for work. Its idealized expectations of spending quality time with loved ones may only make matters worse when family members don't get along, or when some loved ones can't come home for the holidays. And its relentless insistence that it is (as one holiday radio hit claims) "the hap-happiest season of all" can strike those who are sick or grieving or anxious or alone as a tinsel-tinged slap in the face. For many people in pain—physical, emotional, mental, spiritual—Christmas doesn't feel so much crazy as it does crushing.

Don't get me wrong: Our cultural celebrations of Christmas can be a lot of fun. But they tend to ignore that Christmas is, at its core, God's gift to precisely those people who aren't full of holly jolly fa-la-las.

That's why the strange connection between the words *bedlam* and *Bethlehem* might be a good thing. When we think about Bethlehem and that first Christmas, we should remember that more than a little bedlam was involved.

To Whom? To You!

Maybe you've seen Christmas cards that picture the shepherds "living in the fields" of Bethlehem, lounging serenely on a gently rolling hillside among their woolly lambs. Maybe you even played one of the shepherds in a childhood Christmas pageant, bundled up in an old bathrobe or some bed sheets (and practicing ninja moves with your shepherd's staff when the pastor wasn't looking—admit it!).

Well, don't believe it! Our culture sentimentalizes these shepherds the way it sentimentalizes almost everything about the biblical Christmas story. Let's start with the obvious fact: Shepherds, by definition, work with sheep. Sheep are dirty and smelly. That means shepherds are going to get dirty and smelly, too! You wouldn't necessarily want to be stuck under the mistletoe with one of these guys.

In first-century Palestine, "respectable" folk held shepherds at arms' length for more reasons than bad hygiene. Shepherds' work took them far from home, at all hours of the day and night. What's more, shepherds were accused, rightly or wrongly, of letting their flocks graze in other people's fields. Low-class, lazy, louse-infected, lying losers—that's the reputation shepherds often labored under. They had good reason to feel that life was driving them crazy, to say the least.

Any craziness the shepherds experienced, however, didn't keep them from becoming the first folks to hear the good news of Christmas. In fact, God broke into the shepherds' earthbound bedlam with some bedlam on a heavenly scale! That night of Jesus' birth was anything but silent, with a sudden outbreak of divine glory and the appearance of "a great assembly of the heavenly forces" singing the praises of God (**2:13**).

But the cause for all this commotion is where things really get crazy. All this uproar is over the birth of "a newborn baby wrapped snugly and lying in a manger" (**2:12**). And why does this kid rate such a spectacular birth announcement? Because he's "Christ the Lord" (**2:11**). First-century Jews didn't call anyone "Lord" lightly. They didn't even use that title for the Roman Emperor, though he claimed it for himself. No, only one person deserved to be called "Lord": the God of Israel, who chose the family of Abraham and Sarah for a special relationship, freeing them from slavery in Egypt and bringing them to a Promised Land so they could be a blessing to all the families of the world.

So why is this baby's birth worth some heavenly bedlam? Because this same God, the One God whom Israel calls "Lord," is present in him. In Jesus, God has been born into our bedlam, our "craziness." In Jesus, God has been born to real people, facing real problems. As the angel proclaims, "Your savior is born today in David's city" (**2:11**). To you is born in Bethlehem—in bedlam—your Savior!

Keep the "Crazy" in Christmas!

Jesus' birth didn't cause the shepherds' problems to magically disappear, of course. They still had those dirty and smelly sheep to deal with, as well as all the sneering and snide remarks from their neighbors. There's no indication the angels returned for a repeat performance the next night. The first Christmas didn't bust the shepherds out of their bedlam.

But something did change. Luke tells us that, after they visited Jesus in the manger, they "returned home, glorifying and praising God for all they had heard and seen" (**2:20**). In other words they were raising a ruckus, echoing the hoopla they'd heard on high. Now they could face the smelly sheep, nasty neighbors, and every dark night to come with music in their mouths and hope in their hearts. Now they knew they were not alone, for the Lord, the Savior, was born for them in "Bedlam."

That's our song and our hope, too. If we're looking for Christmas to magically make our problems disappear, we're going to be disappointed. But if we're looking to Christ himself, then we can face our problems with more confidence and strength and hope than we can manage on our own.

We may even, like the shepherds, find ourselves making some blessed bedlam when we emerge on the other side of this Christmas season. Not the mindless melodies of the 24-7 Christmas music; not the forced frivolity of holiday parties; and certainly not the ringing of cash register bells. Maybe we'll find ourselves glorifying and praising the God whose foolishness is wiser than human wisdom (see **1 Corinthians 1:25**)—our "crazy" Christ who chooses, for no reason other than love, to be born in and to share our bedlam with us—our surprising Savior who comes down to us so that one day, in his time, he can raise us up to where he is.

[1] From *The Anatomy of Madness: Essays in the History of Psychiatry*, Volume 2, edited by W.F. Bynum, Roy Porter, and Michael Shepherd (Routledge, 1985, 2004); page 29.
[2] From *London: A Biography,* by Peter Ackroyd (Random House Digital, 2009).

❖ ❖ ❖ ❖

Light the Advent Candles

Recruit volunteers to read aloud the following litany, with the entire group responding by saying the boldfaced text.

The Lord be with you!
And also with you!

Leader: You will need an Advent wreath, five wax or electric candles, and hymnals or songbooks including "O Little Town of Bethlehem."

"Who could possibly
   compare to the LORD our God?
   God rules from on high;
   he has to come down
      to even see heaven and earth!" (**Psalm 113:5-6**).

In Jesus Christ, God comes down to see—and to save!

"Jesus isn't ashamed to call [us] brothers and sisters when he
says, . . .
*'Here I am with the children
whom God has given to me.'* . . .
[S]ince the children share in flesh and blood, he also shared the same
things in the same way" (**Hebrews 2:11b, 13b-14a**).

Light one Advent candle.

Great and gracious God, sometimes we let Christmas drive us crazy
   instead of taking time to remember and rejoice that in Jesus' birth,
   you met us in the middle of our loud and chaotic lives,
   promising peace that passes all our understanding.
By your Spirit, center our celebrating on you,
   that we would make a joyful noise about the good news of your
   arrival among us, and for us, in our Savior, Christ the Lord.

Read or sing together "O Little Town of Bethlehem" (Stanza 4); The
United Methodist Hymnal, *230.*

O holy Child of Bethlehem, descend to us, we pray;
Cast out our sin and enter in, be born in us today.
We hear the Christmas angels the great glad tidings tell;
O come to us, abide with us, our Lord Emmanuel!
                                        —WORDS: Phillips Brooks (1868)

Unto us is born in bedlam a Savior!
Thanks be to God!

Exchange words and gestures of peace with one another.

Hear God's Word

Read Luke 2:8-14, then the article for Week One, "A New Word for Madness." Discuss some or all of these questions.

❖ What, if anything, about the Christmas season drives you crazy? How might you make this Christmas a little less crazy?
❖ How, if ever, have you celebrated Christmas when life was hard?
❖ What made life hard for the Bethlehem shepherds that first Christmas? Why was the angelic message in **Luke 2:10-11** especially good news for them?
❖ Whom would you particularly like to know, "Your savior is born today" (**2:11**)? How could you tell and show that person this good news?

Responding to God's Word

Leader: Choose one or more of the following activities.

Make a "Bethlehem Bedlam" Montage

Each person should choose a traditional Christmas image from old cards and/or Christian education materials, along with an image from magazines, newspapers, or the Internet that depicts a difficult circumstance people face. Each participant should then glue or tape the images to the paper to make a montage that illustrates how the angels' news of Jesus' birth is meant for those living in "bedlam."

Leader: You will need old Christmas cards; old Christian education materials about Christmas; magazines and newspapers; scissors; a large sheet of mural paper; glue; markers, crayons, and other art supplies.

Allow time for each person to talk about his or her contribution to the montage, then display the montage for the rest of the congregation to see during the Advent and Christmas seasons.

Shout About the Savior

Write and perform a song, chant, or cheer based on the angels' good news (see **Luke 2:10-14**). Perform your work and (if possible) record it for others in the congregation to hear.

Leader: You will need recording equipment, if possible, for youth to use.

Meet a Messenger

The word *angel* literally means "messenger." Invite someone from your congregation who ministers with people in difficult circumstances (for example, through a homeless shelter, literacy program, children's legal advocacy program, and so forth) to speak with your group about how what they do communicates the angels' message, "Your savior is born" (**2:11**). If it is appropriate, encourage your guest speaker to discuss ways your group can support the ministry.

Leader: Invite someone in your church who ministers to people who face difficult circumstances in life to visit and speak to your youth.

House of Bread

The name *Bethlehem* means, in Hebrew, "house of bread." It's very appropriate that Jesus, who would call himself "the bread of life" (**John 6:35**), was born in the house of bread! To remember and share this truth with others, bake some Christmas bread or cookies with your class. Use a favorite family recipe, or experiment with a new recipe. As you work, ask the following:

Leader: You will need cooking and packaging supplies for the baked goods.

❖ What do we mean when we call Jesus "the bread of life"? (Read **John 6:26-40** for context.)
❖ What are some ways we, as individuals and as a youth ministry, will feed others, physically and spiritually, in the name of the baby born in "the house of bread" this Christmas?

Enjoy the finished product together before packing and distributing the rest to share with homebound or hospitalized members of your congregation.

Daily Devotions

This week think and pray about how God announces good news to people living amid "bedlam," as well as how God might announce that good news through you.

MONDAY: *Genesis 21:9-21*

God had promised old man Abraham and his wife Sarah innumerable descendants, but they were impatient waiting for God to keep that promise. They arranged for Sarah's servant Hagar to give birth to Abraham's first son, Ishmael. When God made good on the promise with Isaac's birth, Abraham and Sarah forced Hagar and Ishmael to leave. What good news does God announce to Hagar and Ishmael? What good news does God have for people today who have been rejected?

TUESDAY: *Exodus 3:1-12*

People who are suffering often fear that God isn't paying attention to them. God's meeting with Moses at the burning bush shows that God does pay attention (**3:7**). Who are the suffering people in your community? Is God telling you to "get going" (**3:10**) and share, through caring acts, the good news that God loves them?

WEDNESDAY: *Isaiah 7:10-16*

We often hear God's promise of the child Immanuel applied to Jesus. While Christians believe Jesus is "God with us" in a unique way, Isaiah's prophecy meant something different. Through Isaiah, God urged Israel's king to sit tight and trust God. The danger he feared from an enemy empire would pass in the time it took a newborn baby to begin eating solid food and telling right from wrong (**7:14-16**). When does fear make it difficult for you to trust God? Who are God's messengers of good news for you when you're afraid?

THURSDAY: Ezekiel 1:1-21

Talk about bedlam! Ezekiel's vision may seem like crazy special effects from a sci-fi blockbuster, but it's actually a visual promise of God's presence. The mighty Babylonian empire had conquered Jerusalem and destroyed the Temple, the place above all places where Jews expected to encounter God. Those wild, whirling wheels Ezekiel sees reassure God's people, living in exile, that God isn't limited to just one locale. God is with them even when they're far from home. How do you feel knowing that God is always with you? How will you communicate God's presence to people who have no home?

FRIDAY: Mark 6:34-44

Jesus' compassion for people meant he was concerned with not only their spiritual needs but also their physical needs. The need to eat is one of our most basic needs, and hunger has always been one of humanity's most pressing problems. In this story Jesus provides a miraculous meal—but it starts with the five loaves and two fish gathered by his disciples. Today, share your food with someone who is hungry.

SATURDAY: Acts 16:25-34

Imprisoned for their missionary preaching about Jesus, the apostle Paul and his partner Silas received a miraculous "message"—in God's actions, not in words—of freedom in the middle of a dark night, a lot like the shepherds of Bethlehem did. How have you heard and seen God's good news in the darkness of your life or someone else's life? During this Christmas season, how will you share God's good news with people in physical or spiritual prisons?

WEEK TWO

Freedom

Galatians 5:13-15

You were called to freedom, brothers and sisters;
only don't let this freedom be an opportunity to indulge
your selfish impulses, but serve each other through love.
All the Law has been fulfilled in a single statement:
Love your neighbor as yourself.
But if you bite and devour each other, be careful that you
don't get eaten up by each other!

Trapped in the Twilight Zone

One of my favorite "Christmas traditions" is actually a New Year's one: the Syfy Channel's annual *Twilight Zone* marathon. One episode I always enjoy catching is "Nick of Time," starring the one and only William Shatner—Captain Kirk/Denny Crane/the Priceline Negotiator!

Shatner plays Don Carter, who is eating with his wife in a diner that has penny-operated "fortune telling" machines on its tables. Drop in your coin, ask a "yes-or-no" question, and get a tiny card with a vague message. Don is superstitious and begins to believe the machine can accurately forecast the future. He spends hour after hour and penny after penny asking the "Mystic Seer" questions. His wife tries to persuade him that the machine's "predictions" are simple coincidences, but Don is gripped by the belief that the tabletop toy will show his way forward in life.

In case you've never seen the show, I won't spoil the ending. But right up to its final moments, "Nick of Time" asks how we'll live. As *Twilight Zone* creator Rod Serling says in his closing voiceover, we can choose to live "with confidence," or we can allow ourselves to be "permanently enslaved by the tyranny of fear and superstition, facing the future with a kind of helpless dread."

In Control—or Controlled?

Let's face it: Life is often messy, risky, scary business. Even if we're not superstitious, we all rely on something to help us cope with our fears about the future and anxieties about the present. Maybe we reassure ourselves that we're in control by turning to complicated customs, or determined self-disciplines, or rigid rules. I'm not saying all rules, rituals, or routines are bad. But sometimes those very structures cause their own kind of craziness. We may find ourselves working so hard to keep our lives in order that we don't see just how disordered our lives have become.

A girl in my high school—let's call her Liz—had moved to town with her family just before the beginning of the school year. She was unhappy at leaving behind her old school and friends. All Liz thought she had left was her love of running. She decided that, if she couldn't control anything else, she could at least control that.

This decision might have been OK, but it led to choices that weren't. Liz started running when she was supposed to be elsewhere; for example, she'd take quick, light jogs around her new church's neighborhood when her parents thought she was sitting in Sunday school. And her desire to stay physically fit, not bad in itself, turned into a fixation on her weight. She was convinced that no boy at school would ever give her a second look because she was fat (she wasn't). Her initial choice to purge what she ate became a compulsion. Liz secretly suffered from bulimia for about a year before, thankfully, she confided in her track coach, who helped get her into treatment and her whole family into therapy.

I'll never fully know exactly what Liz went through, or why. It's not easy to explain eating disorders. But I think I see in Liz's very real experience something like Don Carter's fictional one. As psychologist Dr. Susan Albers writes, "Eating disorders take hold of someone's mind and just won't let go . . . [An] eating disorder offers . . . a false sense of protection . . . [and] a temporary way to cope with life."[1] Both Don on TV and Liz at my high school found themselves captive to situations that, in their beginning, had looked like paths to empowerment and freedom.

Paul's "Christmas Letter"

None of this sounds much like Christmas, right? Certainly not if we're expecting holly jolly ho-ho-hos. But if we believe the message the angels shouted to those shepherds—that to us is born "in bedlam" a Savior—then we'll realize that Jesus came for people like Liz and Don and you and me, people whose efforts to cope with and control our lives have instead led us into captivity.

In all the letters he wrote to early Christians, the apostle Paul never taught them to celebrate Jesus' birthday. But in his letter to believers in Galatia, Paul did directly mention Jesus' birth. Unlike annual holiday epistles full of news about what we've been up to, however, Paul's "Christmas letter" is about what God was up to when Jesus was born— "born through a woman, and born under the Law" (**Galatians 4:4**)—and what we should be up to as a result.

When Paul writes to the Galatians, he is furious. Some of Paul's flashier, smoother-talking rival preachers have bamboozled the Galatians into thinking that, by keeping all the right rules, they can control not just their lives but even their relationship with God. They've been gripped by the thought that perfectly keeping every commandment in the Law is the way forward.

Paul understands that no determined self-disciplines or rigid rules lead to abundant life. This letter is his attempt to grab the Galatians by their shoulders and, with his words, shake them into seeing just how disordered their "Law-ordered" lives have become. He tells the Galatians that if they truly want to move forward, if they truly want to be free, they must give up whatever control they think they have and trust Jesus alone. Jesus was born to put them right with God. Don't make the mistake of believing that the Christian life is about "you" getting yourself together. It's not. It's about God getting you together, through and in the Son! "I have been crucified with Christ," says Paul, "and I no longer live, but Christ lives in me. And the life that I now live in my body, I live by faith, indeed, by the faithfulness of God's Son, who loved me and gave himself for me" (**2:19-20**).

The birth of Jesus Christ is a key stage in God's radical rescue plan. In Jesus, God breaks into all the prisons we've built for ourselves in order to break us out. "Christ has set us free for freedom," writes Paul. "Therefore stand firm and don't submit to the bondage of slavery again" (**5:1**).

Freedom to Serve

There's something funny about freedom in Christ—some people might even call it "crazy." Jesus doesn't set us free to do whatever we want, whenever we want, however we want. Isn't that how we got into trouble in the first place, acting as though we were in control? Jesus loves us too much to let us fall into that trap again!

Paul clarifies: "You were called to freedom . . . only don't let this freedom be an opportunity to indulge your selfish impulses, but serve each other through love" (**5:13**). Paul reminds his readers there's only one rule worth keeping: "*Love your neighbor as yourself*" (**5:14**; see **Leviticus 19:18**). And, as Jesus himself taught, when we do that, we're loving God, too (see **Matthew 22:34-40**).

There's another *Twilight Zone* episode that airs in each New Year's marathon, a story set on Christmas Eve. In "The Night of the Meek," Henry Corwin is a department store Santa Claus who shows up drunk for work. The manager fires him. Still in his dingy Saint Nick suit, Henry roams the streets with nowhere to go and nothing to do until he finds a magic sack that produces any gift anyone wishes. Henry spends Christmas Eve delighting everyone from hard-nosed police officers to wide-eyed little children with wonderful presents. When the bag seems empty, Henry wishes he could make people so happy every year. He turns a corner—and finds an elf with a sleigh and reindeer, waiting to take him to the North Pole. Henry has been freed from the prison of his drinking in order to take up a life of serving others by bringing them joy.

Faith in Jesus isn't magic. Leaving our prisons can take time and hard work and never happens in a moment. But it also doesn't happen without the power of God, present with us in Jesus Christ. Through his Spirit, Jesus strengthens and sustains us to trust him more than we trust ourselves and to follow the way of loving service that he has shown us.

[1] Dr. Susan Albers, "The Reason An Eating Disorder Can Hold You Captive,"
1 September 2009 (*http://www.psychologytoday.com/blog/comfort-cravings/200909/
the-reason-eating-disorder-can-hold-you-captive*), paras. 5, 7.

❖   ❖   ❖   ❖

Light the Advent Candles

Recruit several youth to read aloud the following litany, with the entire group responding by saying the boldfaced text.

Leader: You will need an Advent wreath, five wax or electric candles, and hymnals or songbooks including "Go, Tell It on the Mountain."

The Lord be with you!
And also with you!

"Let [us] thank the LORD
  for his faithful love
  and his wondrous works for all people
because God has shattered bronze doors and split iron bars in two!"
(Psalm 107:15-16).

In Jesus Christ, God comes down and sets us free to serve!

"If you were raised with Christ, look for the things that are above where Christ is sitting at God's right side. . . . You died, and your life is hidden with Christ in God. When Christ, who is your life, is revealed, then you also will be revealed with him in glory" (**Colossians 3:1, 3-4**).

Light two Advent candles.

> You created us for freedom, God; but we forget, so easily and so often,
>   that we are only free when we are trusting you.
> Forgive us when we think that we are in control, and when we act as
>   though we can save ourselves.
> Show us how to live in true freedom that comes through faith in you,
>   so confident that we are secure in your hands
> that we fearlessly open our hands to others in the name of our Savior,
>   your Son, Jesus Christ.

Read or sing together "Go, Tell It on the Mountain" (Stanza 3); The United Methodist Hymnal, *251.*

> **Down in a lowly manger the humble Christ was born,**
> **and God sent us salvation that blessed Christmas morn.**
> **Go, tell it on the mountain, over the hills and everywhere;**
> **go, tell it on the mountain, that Jesus Christ is born.**
> —WORDS: John W. Work, Jr. (1907)

Unto us is born in bedlam a Savior!
Thanks be to God!

Exchange words and gestures of peace with one another.

Hear God's Word

Read Galatians 5:13-15, then the article for Week Two, "Trapped in the Twilight Zone." Discuss some or all of the following questions.

❖ How superstitious are you? When have you believed, or been tempted to believe, in the power of a superstition? What happened?

❖ In what ways should we want to be "in control" of our lives, and in what ways should we accept that we are not?

❖ How did the early Christians in Galatia misunderstand and misuse God's law?

❖ Why is it important to know that Jesus was born as a real human being: "born through a woman, and born under the Law" (**Galatians 4:4**)?

❖ How is the way that God defines freedom different from how human beings often define freedom?

❖ According to Paul, what are the consequences of abusing our Christian freedom (**5:15**)?

Responding to God's Word

Leader: Choose one or more of the following activities.

Paraphrasing Paul

Sometimes trying to write ideas from Scripture in our own words can help us understand them better. On a separate piece of paper, write Paul's point in **Galatians 5:13-15** using your own words or in words that would be easy for people of your generation to understand.

Lectio Divina

Lectio divina means "divine" or "spiritual reading." It is an ancient way of listening for God's message in Scripture. Ask three different persons to read aloud **Galatians 5:13-15**. During the first reading, everyone should listen for a word or phrase that catches his or her attention. After each reading, pause for a brief time of silence, then ask the appropriate question below. Invite those who wish to do so to respond aloud to the questions. There are no right or wrong answers; the exercise is an opportunity to practice paying close attention to how God uses the Bible to speak to us.

❖ *After the first reading*: What word, phrase, or image from the Scripture most attracts your attention?

❖ *After the second reading*: How does this Scripture connect with your life today?

❖ *After the third reading*: What specific action might God be calling you to take in response to this Scripture?

Sympathy With the Imprisoned

Jesus calls for compassion toward people in prison in **Matthew 25:36**, and the Letter to the Hebrews commends readers for having practiced it (**10:34**). The Christmas season often presents special opportunities to show concern for those in prison and their families.

Leader: Ahead of time check out the Prison Fellowship's Angel Tree website along with prison mail regulations.

Consider making and sending to prison inmates Christmas cards containing messages of God's love (check with prisons regarding mail regulations), or plan a gift collection for inmates' children through such ministries as Prison Fellowship's Angel Tree (see *http://www.prisonfellowship.org/programs/angel-tree/*).

Breaking Chains

Each participant should write or draw on one or more strips of paper a description of someone or something that holds people captive, literally or metaphorically. Then link the paper strips together (interlocking circles closed on the ends with tape). When the chain is finished, gather in a circle with everyone holding the chain. Then ask:

Leader: You will need invisible tape and small strips of construction paper (approximately 6 to 8 inches by 1 inch), enough for each youth to have one or two.

❖ What are some ways you identified that people are held captive?

❖ How can we support people who are captive in these situations?

❖ How is God at work to bring these people to freedom?

Lead a brief prayer for people who are captive in these and other circumstances. Then say together: "Christ has set us free for freedom!" (**Galatians 5:1**), as you break apart the paper chain.

Daily Devotions

This week think and pray about the freedom that Jesus brings. Gaining an overview of Paul's letter to the Galatians will help you appreciate the brief passages that we read together in this session.

MONDAY: Galatians 1:13-16

Paul begins his letter by reminding readers that he used to follow all the right rules just as they are trying to follow them. His concern about keeping the rules actually led him to oppose the early church. How can being too tied to rules, routines, and traditions keep us from recognizing and responding to God?

TUESDAY: Galatians 2:11-16

Paul was upset with Cephas (another name for Peter) because, while Cephas felt free in Christ to stop observing Jewish dietary laws when eating with non-Jews, he was insisting that non-Jewish converts to Christianity observe the Torah. Why is it often easy to hold other people to stricter standards than we hold ourselves? When have you been guilty of hypocrisy in your faith?

WEDNESDAY: Galatians 3:6-12

Paul's point in these verses is that God did not choose to bless Abraham because of anything Abraham did. Instead, Abraham's blessings were a result of his steady faith, even when tested. In what ways are you tempted to rely on what you can do more than what God does? Stop now to think about and offer thanks for all God has freely given you.

THURSDAY: Galatians 3:23-25

Paul argues that, with Jesus' coming, our relationship to God's law changes. It is no longer what keeps us living in the right way.

Instead, our faith in Jesus keeps us right with God. What rules did you have to obey as a child that you no longer have to obey? As you have grown in your faith in Jesus, how have your religious practices changed to reflect your freedom in him?

FRIDAY: Galatians 3:26-28

The truth that our baptism makes visible, that we belong to Jesus Christ, takes priority over every other way in which we identify ourselves. What does Paul mean when he teaches that differences in ethnicity, gender, and social status no longer matter in Christ? How does this truth free us to look at other people in new ways?

SATURDAY: Galatians 5:22-26

Paul highlights attitudes that demonstrate the presence and activity of the Holy Spirit in a person's life. Is there someone you know who truly follows the Spirit by demonstrating the Spirit's fruit (see verses 22–25)?

WEEK THREE

Superhero

Matthew 11:1-6

When Jesus finished teaching his twelve disciples,
he went on from there to teach and preach in their cities.
Now when John heard in prison about the things
Jesus was doing, he sent word by his disciples to Jesus,
asking, "Are you the one who is to come, or should
we look for another?"
Jesus responded, "Go, report to John what you hear
and see. Those who were blind are able to see.
Those who were crippled are walking. People with skin
diseases are cleansed. Those who were deaf now hear.
Those who were dead are raised up. The poor have good
news proclaimed to them. Happy are those who don't
stumble and fall because of me."

Super Santa!

Is Santa Claus a superhero? The question may not be a crazy one!

Peter Coogan earned his Ph.D. studying superhero stories. (Don't you wish you could do that for school credit?) In his book *Superhero: The Secret Origin of a Genre* (Copyright © 2006 Peter Coogan; MonkeyBrain Books), Dr. Coogan identifies three traits essential to every superhero: They have a selfless mission in the service of all that is good and right; they actively champion noble causes and high ideals. You know, "truth, justice, and the American way"—that kind of thing. They have special powers that enable them to carry out that mission: flight, super-speed, invulnerability. And they have a unique identity, usually summed up in a codename and costume. No one wearing lightning-streaked spandex and calling himself The Flash, for instance, is going to be the world's slowest man! Superheroes become icons, living symbols of the power and purpose that define them.

Dr. Coogan doesn't say anything about Santa, but I think jolly old Saint Nick fits this superheroic bill pretty well. He's certainly a man with a mission: rewarding virtue and punishing vice, bringing toys to the children on his "nice list" while doling out coal to kiddos who've been naughty. He's got special powers: Surely soaring around the world in a magic reindeer-driven sleigh and shimmying down everyone's chimney in a single night qualify as special powers. And his iconic identity is secure: He embodies generosity, kindness, and joy (for the kids on the "nice list," at least!). People who would never wear a Superman or Batman T-shirt will, during the holidays, gladly wear a Santa hat—and for the same reason—to connect with the qualities the character embodies.

That, of course, is one more way in which Santa is a superhero—he's a character. He's a wish-fulfillment fantasy who is no more real than Spider-Man, Wonder Woman, or Wolverine. I know, Santa's real in "the spirit of giving is real" sense. But that's what my mom told me when she was trying to make me feel better after I learned the Santa secret. No one leaves cookies and milk out for the spirit of giving—where's the fun in that? You may or may not consider Santa a superhero; but you've got to admit, on the level of the literally real, he is, like them, a super no-show.

Waiting for a Super Savior?

I wonder if John the Baptist expected the Messiah to storm onto the scene like a superheroic Santa. It might account for the question he asks Jesus, one that seems pretty puzzling at first: "Are you the one who is to come, or should we look for another?" (**Matthew 11:3**).

Some readers think this question was John's clever way to get his own disciples to give Jesus a hearing and decide to follow him instead. But I don't think it's too tough to figure out why John might have had doubts. He's in prison—not one of the metaphorical prisons we talked about last week, but the real deal, with chains and iron bars.

While down in Herod's dungeon, I bet John thought a lot about the times when people "from Jerusalem, throughout Judea, and all around the Jordan River" (**3:5**) heard him calling for repentance and answered in droves. John baptized those who confessed their sins in the river's waters, readying them for God's revelation of the Messiah. John preached about a powerful enforcer who'd sort the good from the bad, "the wheat from the husks" (**3:12**)—the "naughty" from the "nice!" This hero on the horizon would judge a sinful world, in God's name and with God's authority, "with the Holy Spirit and with fire" (**3:11**). The Messiah would save the day by shouldering God's wrathful ax and chopping down every fruitless, faithless obstacle to God's will being done on earth as it is in heaven. He'd reduce all God's enemies to kindling for a holy bonfire. "Even now," John warned, "the ax is lying at the root of the trees" (**3:10**, NRSV)!

But now John may have been fighting off fears that the Messiah he'd waited for was, like Superman or Santa Claus, just a fantasy. And so he sent word to Jesus, asking him: Is it you? Or, is the Messiah just a character who is a super no-show?

Super Love

Jesus told John's disciples to tell John what they saw and heard Jesus doing. We might look at what Jesus had been up to and think, *Sounds superheroic to me!* Jesus was giving sight to eyes that were blind and hearing to ears that were deaf. He was healing legs that had been rendered useless and cleansing skin that was sick. He was even raising the dead!

But Jesus wasn't the only wonder-worker in first-century Palestine. Other ancient texts tell about claims of healers and miracle-makers. Jesus did some amazing deeds, but he wanted John—and us—to focus on the meaning of those deeds. Maybe that's why Jesus mentioned last, as if emphasizing it the most, that he was proclaiming good news to the poor. That action is a clue to understanding the others. Jesus came as a Messiah less interested in beating up bad guys (or even leaving coal in their stockings) than in embodying the good news of God's light-bringing, life-giving love.

❖ **Love is Jesus' mission.** The Son of God entered this world for no reason but love for his Father and for us, the sinners his Father sent him to save (see **John 3:16**). Jesus freely accepted that mission, staying "obedient to the point of death, even death on a cross" (**Philippians 2:8**).

❖ **Love is Jesus' power.** Jesus loved us "fully" (**John 13:1**), more perfectly and powerfully than anyone else could. Jesus' love is the only love that never fails.

❖ **Love is Jesus' identity.** Jesus held broken bread and called it his body; he poured out wine and called it his blood. When he appeared to his disciples on the first Easter Day, "he showed them his hands and feet" (**Luke 24:40**) and the scars from his crucifixion. The wounds Jesus suffered in love for us represent the power and purpose that define him.

Everything Jesus did revealed the love that led him to the cross: The physical healings he granted foreshadowed the complete healing he would offer to all people. The raising of a few dead people anticipated the eternal life to which he raises all who believe in him. And his companionship with the poor looked forward to their promised inheritance of God's kingdom and to the great day when all who are hungry will be fed, all who weep will rejoice, and all who are captive will be set free.

How do you think John reacted when his disciples reported back? Did he keep on waiting for a superheroic Santa-style savior? Did he keep wondering why Jesus didn't bring in God's kingdom right then and there? Or did John see and hear what his disciples had—that, in Jesus, the real Savior had shown up after all?

Subverting the Status Quo

In his study of superheroes, Dr. Coogan points out that superheroes rarely actually change anything. Yes, their stories usually end with bad guys being defeated; but when superheroes fight only to restore order as it was before the villains unleashed their latest schemes, they "reinforce the idea that things are the way they should be" (*Superhero,* page 237).

John's expectations of the Messiah may have been misguided, but he was right about this: Things aren't the way they should be. All kinds of bedlam still bear down on us: sickness, grief, poverty, anger, crime, and war, to name a few. Like John we may wonder, "If Jesus is the Messiah, why doesn't he just swoop in and save the day already?"

Jesus wasn't angry with John for questioning, and he won't be angry with us, either. But he also won't concede the unspoken assumption of those questions—that he has been idle. He hasn't been. He told his disciples that he was busy doing the works of God who sent him (see **John 9:4**), and he still is. He challenges us to look for the sights and sounds of his activity. He shows us what he's doing, and he calls us to join in the work. In effect, Jesus asks us: *Are you the one I've been looking for?*

Are we superheroes? Of course not. But does Jesus give us a new identity, a mission, and the power of his Holy Spirit to fulfill it? That question may not be a crazy one!

Light the Advent Candles

Recruit several youth to read aloud the following litany, with the entire group responding by saying the boldfaced text.

Leader: *You will need an Advent wreath, five wax or electric candles, and hymnals or songbooks including "Joy to the World."*

The Lord be with you!
And also with you!

"Those who honor the LORD,
who adore God's commandments, are truly happy! . . .

They shine in the dark for others who do right.
They are merciful, compassionate, and righteous.
Those who lend generously are good people—
    as are those who conduct their affairs with justice.
Yes, these sorts of people will never be shaken;
    the righteous will be remembered forever!" (**Psalm 112:1, 4-6**).

In Jesus Christ, God comes down and commissions us to do the work of God's kingdom!

"[W]e are God's accomplishment, created in Christ Jesus to do good things. God planned for these good things to be the way that we live our lives" (**Ephesians 2:10**).

Light three Advent candles.

We confess, O God, how easy it is to look at our world and our lives
    and see only what is wrong.
Open our eyes to glimpses of where you are even now at work—
    comforting those who are sad, strengthening those who are weak,
    renewing the hopes of those who are hopeless,
    opening new possibilities for those who face dead ends.
Give us the will and the courage to be the ones through whom you
    work, faithful followers of your Son, our Savior, Jesus Christ.

Read or sing together "Joy to the World" (Stanza 4); The United Methodist Hymnal, *246.*

**He rules the world with truth and grace,
and makes the nations prove the glories of his righteousness,
and wonders of his love, and wonders of his love,
and wonders, wonders of his love.**

—Words: Isaac Watts (1719)

Unto us is born in bedlam a Savior!
Thanks be to God!

Exchange words and gestures of peace with one another.

Hear God's Word

Read Matthew 11:1-6, then the article for Week Three, "Super Santa!"
Discuss some or all of the following questions.

❖ How and why do people (maybe even, sometimes, you) expect
   Jesus to be like a superhero, or like Santa Claus? Why is it wrong
   to think about Jesus in this way?

❖ When has Jesus shown you who he is in a new and surprising way?

❖ Read these prophecies from the Book of Isaiah: **Isaiah 26:19-21;
   29:18-21; 35:3-6a**. How do these passages help us understand
   what Jesus says to John's disciples?

❖ John may have been disappointed that Jesus wasn't the superheroic
   messiah he'd expected. When have you felt disappointed in the
   way God has done something?

❖ John knew that things weren't the way they should be during his
   lifetime. What wrong thing in the world today, or in your life,
   troubles you most? What have you done, or what could you do, to
   make it better? How do you pray about this problem?

Responding to God's Word

Leader: *Choose one or more of the following activities.*

Your Not-So-Secret Identity

Jesus told us not to boast about how we serve him (see **Luke 17:9-10**).
But just for fun, in keeping with the theme of this week's article, design a
"superhero" identity for yourself that represents something you do or will
commit to doing to love others in Jesus' name. Choose a catchy codename
for yourself; design a costume (be sure to include a visual element that
symbolizes what you are doing); and sketch a scene that shows you in
action! Combine your drawing with others' and publish a "comic book"
for distribution within your congregation or on your church's website.

Gathering Good News

It doesn't always grab the headlines the way bad news does, but good news is out there to "hear and see" (**Matthew 11:4**), and Jesus calls us to listen and look for it. Check recent issues of your local newspaper and/or news websites for

Leader: You will need a copy of your local newspaper and/or access to Internet.

at least one article you think points to Jesus' activity in the world today. Talk briefly with the rest of your group about why you chose the article(s) you did. (You can also find good news stories, including several featuring how Jesus is at work through youth today, through United Methodist TV— *http://www.youtube.com/user/UnitedMethodistTV*—or other denominational websites.)

Impromptu Interview

One way we can learn to recognize Jesus at work is to ask others how they see Jesus at work. Take a video camera or mobile device with video-recording capability to your congregation's coffee hour or other social gathering, or station yourself outside the sanctuary after a worship service. Ask those who are willing to answer on-camera the question, "Where do you hear and see Jesus at work today?" Edit responses into a video presentation for use in your congregation or on your church website.

Daily Devotions

This week think and pray about ways in which your life can offer evidence that people hear and see as they look for signs that God is at work today.

MONDAY: *Genesis 33:10*

Esau had plenty of reason to be mad at his scheming younger brother, Jacob. Jacob swindled Esau out of his birthright and their father Isaac's blessing. Esau had been so furious that Jacob ran for his life. Jacob came back years later, fully expecting to confront a still-angry Esau—but Esau embraced and forgave him. Is there someone you can meet with peace and forgiveness, as Esau met Jacob, so that your face, too, can reflect the face of God?

TUESDAY: *Leviticus 19:33-34*

Sometimes Christians forget that God's commandment to love others doesn't first appear in the New Testament and that it extends to people who may be different from ourselves. According to these verses, what motive do God's people have for loving strangers? What can you do today to love strangers in God's name?

WEDNESDAY: *Luke 3:7-14*

John the Baptist didn't preach that people should sit around doing nothing while they waited for the Messiah to come. In these verses, what practical steps does he call people to take that can be seen as signs of God at work?

THURSDAY: *Matthew 25:34-40*

Jesus' words about how we can find and serve him aren't difficult to understand, but they can be difficult to put into practice. Notice that "those who are righteous" (verse 37) aren't even aware of what they've done. Living with Jesus' love has become second nature to them. Today, practice doing at least one thing (from this Scripture) that Jesus commands us to do, remembering that, when you do it for one of the least, you're doing it for him.

FRIDAY: 1 Timothy 2:1-4

Sometimes we don't think of prayer as actually "doing something," but these verses teach otherwise. How can praying for other people, especially leaders, be a way of loving them? Spend time today praying for those in authority as they work to find solutions for the problems in our world.

SATURDAY: 1 Corinthians 13

The apostle Paul makes it clear that some of the most "super"-sounding deeds we can think of, when accomplished without love, aren't so "super" at all. Spend some time reflecting on the attributes of love that Paul lists in verses 4-7. When have you experienced this kind of love? How can you demonstrate this kind of love during this Advent and Christmas season?

WEEK FOUR

Remembrance

Luke 2:1-20

In those days Caesar Augustus declared that everyone
throughout the empire should be enrolled in the tax lists.
This first enrollment occurred when Quirinius governed
Syria. Everyone went to their own cities to be enrolled.
Since Joseph belonged to David's house and family line,
he went up from the city of Nazareth in Galilee to David's
city, called Bethlehem, in Judea. He went to be enrolled
together with Mary, who was promised to him in marriage
and who was pregnant. While they were there,
the time came for Mary to have her baby. She gave birth to
her firstborn child, a son, wrapped him snugly,
and laid him in a manger, because there was no
place for them in the guestroom.

Nearby shepherds were living in the fields,
guarding their sheep at night. The Lord's angel stood
before them, the Lord's glory shone around them,
and they were terrified.
The angel said, "Don't be afraid! Look! I bring good news
to you—wonderful, joyous news for all people.
Your savior is born today in David's city. He is Christ the
Lord. This is a sign for you: you will find a newborn baby
wrapped snugly and lying in a manger."
Suddenly a great assembly of the heavenly forces was
with the angel praising God. They said,
"Glory to God in heaven, and on earth peace among
those whom he favors."
When the angels returned to heaven, the shepherds said
to each other, "Let's go right now to Bethlehem
and see what's happened. Let's confirm what the Lord
has revealed to us. They went quickly and found Mary
and Joseph, and the baby lying in the manger. When they
saw this, they reported what they had been told about
this child. Everyone who heard it was amazed at what the
shepherds told them. Mary committed these things
to memory and considered them carefully.
The shepherds returned home, glorifying and praising
God for all they had heard and seen.
Everything happened just as they had been told.

What's Your First Christmas Memory?

I have a theory about Christmas. I theorize that our enjoyment of Christmas is directly proportional to the extent to which our earliest Christmas memory is positive or negative.

On a scale of 1 to 10—where 10 is "I wish it were Christmas every day" and 1 is "365 days until next Christmas is 3,000 days too few"—how would you rate your attitude toward the holiday? Now, what's your earliest Christmas memory? My hunch is that people who can't get enough of Christmas—the "10's," the folks who start putting Christmas carols on their mp3 players as soon as Halloween is over, or who actually want to be seen in public wearing those holiday sweatshirts with sewn-on blinking Christmas bulbs—have a delightful first Christmas memory; while the people who have had enough of Christmas—the "1's," who shut off the porch light when carolers wander into their neighborhood, or who secretly root for the Grinch whenever viewing that classic cartoon on TV—have a dreadful first memory.

My first memory of Christmas is mixed, which may account for the ambiguity I feel toward the whole season. When I was four years old, way back in 1976, what I wanted most for Christmas was a Six Million Dollar Man doll. (That's right: doll. *Star Wars* wouldn't hit theaters until 1977, so its merchandise hadn't yet introduced the concept of "action figure.") I dutifully scrawled a letter to Santa, but worried that I had about as much chance of getting the gift I wanted as Bigfoot had of beating Steve Austin (the bionic man). I don't remember what I'd done wrong, but I do remember fearing it might have been enough to land me on Santa's "naughty" list. I felt shame as I handed my letter over to Mom (I suppose she'd offered to "mail it to the North Pole" for me). Yuletide angst must have been all over my face because she asked me, "Michael, what's wrong?" I told her I was afraid I'd been too bad for Santa to bring me that doll. She gave me a big hug and said that she was pretty sure Santa would bring me the Six Million Dollar Man. And, sure enough, there he was beneath the tree on Christmas morning.

On the one hand, it's not a bad memory as first Christmas memories go. I mean, my Christmas wish came true, right? But on the other hand, my early experience of Santa-induced anxiety can still rankle me whenever I hear folks singing that I'd better watch out, he's coming to town! I've been accused of being a Scrooge where Santa's concerned. Perhaps I am.

Christmas, like no other time of year, is tangled up with our memories like last year's tree lights. Whether those memories are good or bad, precious or painful (or perhaps some of each) shapes how we do or don't celebrate the holiday.

Mary's "First Christmas" Memory

The Bible doesn't often reveal what the people in its stories were thinking and feeling—so when it does, we probably should pay attention!

Case in point: Luke tells us about Jesus' mother Mary's "first Christmas memory." Of course, she surely remembered a lot about that first Christmas, and not all of it pleasant: the tough travel from Nazareth to Bethlehem (the two towns are about eighty miles apart, and Mary and Joseph couldn't just hop on a commuter train), or the crush of the crowds once they arrived, leaving "no place for them" (**Luke 2:7**). But new mothers often say that those first moments spent cradling their new baby in their arms puts the discomfort of pregnancy and the pain of labor in perspective. It's reasonable to assume Mary felt the same way.

We don't have to assume, however, that those Bethlehem shepherds made an impression on Mary, because Luke tells us they did! When the shepherds relayed what they'd heard about the infant Jesus, "Mary treasured all these words and pondered them in her heart" (**2:19**, NRSV). I bet she did! The shepherds told her that angels had called her baby boy a Savior, the Messiah, and the Lord! What mother wouldn't cherish the memory of hearing her baby called such amazing names?

But Mary didn't just relive the shepherds' report over and over. She tried to make sense out of it. She spent time prayerfully sorting it out and putting it all together. It wouldn't be the last time, either. In the only story in the Bible about Jesus as a youth, his mother responds to his insistence that she should have known he'd be in the Temple by "cherish[ing] every word in her heart" (**2:51**), tucking them away to turn over at a later time, sifting through them for significance. And the more she sifted and searched, pondered and puzzled, the more she believed that God was at work in and through her son in a special way.

Mary seems to have known that memories can be much more than mere mental storage and recall of information about our past. They can be ways to encounter God. Her Christmas memories made her more aware of what God was doing in the present. God wants us to develop that same awareness. It's what can make memories (even, sometimes, painful ones) truly precious.

Making Christmases to Remember

Ultimately, whether your Christmas memories—the first one, or the ones that came later—are positive or negative is beside the point. I don't mean that your memories don't matter. They do! In fact, they matter so much that God wants to breathe the Holy Spirit into them and use them to encourage your growth as a follower of Jesus.

If we're not careful, though, memories of Christmases past—good or bad—can slow that growth. If we allow the Christmases we knew as kids to become the standard by which we measure all our present and future celebrations, we're setting ourselves up not only for disappointment but also for failure in discipleship. Giving to others, for example, isn't a huge part of many little kids' Christmases. Kids generally focus on the gifts they're going to get. That's all right for a four-year-old, but Jesus demands more from us as we mature. In contrast, if we push away Christmas today because some of yesterday's Christmases disappointed us, even grieved or wounded us, we might be missing out on ways Jesus can use the celebration of his birth now to surprise us with peace, hope, and joy. I eventually dealt with my Santa syndrome, for instance, and took my mom's little lesson in grace to the next level: I have skipped the Santa game with my kids. They know their presents come from real people who love them no matter what, "naughty or nice."

As much as God can and does meet us in our memories, though, God also says, "Don't remember the prior things; don't ponder ancient history. Look! I'm doing a new thing" (**Isaiah 43:18-19**). It's not that God wants us to become amnesiacs and forget the past. It's that God calls us to develop a special kind of memory, the kind that happens whenever we gather around the table or come to the altar where Jesus invites us to share a loaf and a cup in remembrance of him.

Whatever we remember or don't about past Christmases, I think God's more concerned that we make this Christmas, and all those to come, worth remembering! So do something this Christmas you think will bring you closer to Christ. We can't, of course, schedule a heightened experience of God; we can't guarantee we'll look back someday on any given activity and say, "Oh, now I see what God was up to!" But we can do something. We can put ourselves in God's way. We can make ourselves available to God, as Mary did. We can seek out ways to give to and share with and love other people, and our encounters with them may just turn out to be encounters with the One whose birth we're celebrating.

Light the Advent Candles

Recruit several youth to read aloud the following litany, with the entire group responding by saying the boldfaced text.

Leader: You will need an Advent wreath, five wax or electric candles, and hymnals or songbooks including "O Sing a Song of Bethlehem."

The Lord be with you!
And also with you!

"I will remember the LORD's deeds;
    yes, I will remember your wondrous acts
    from times long past. . . .
God, your way is holiness!
    Who is as great a god as you, God?
You are the God who works wonders;
    you have demonstrated your strength among all peoples"
(Psalm 77:11, 13-14).

In Jesus Christ, God comes down and makes miracles out of our memories!

"Jesus Christ is the same yesterday, today, and forever!" **(Hebrews 13:8).**

Light four Advent candles.

> God of all time, you are always calling us to face your future,
>   but we admit we are preoccupied with the past.
> We get caught up in nostalgia, wishing things could be the way they
>   once were;
> or we avoid our memories of what has been, failing to find out
>   how you were with us.
> As your Holy Spirit hovered over the waters of creation,
> may your Spirit hover over our memories, calling order out of
>   disorder, and out of darkness, light.
> Keep us from either idolizing or demonizing our memories.
> Strengthen us, like Mary, to instead meditate on them,
> marking how you have led us yesterday and resolving to follow you
>   today and throughout all our tomorrows, as faithful disciples of
>   Jesus Christ.

Read or sing together "O Sing a Song of Bethlehem" (Stanza 1); The
United Methodist Hymnal, *179.*

> **O sing a song of Bethlehem, of shepherds watching there,**
> **and of the news that came to them from angels in the air.**
> **The light that shone on Bethlehem fills all the world today;**
> **of Jesus' birth and peace on earth the angels sing alway.**
>   —WORDS: Louis F. Benson (1889)

Unto us is born in bedlam a Savior!
Thanks be to God!

Exchange words and gestures of peace with one another.

Hear God's Word

Read Luke 2:1-20, then the article for Week Four, "What's Your First Christmas Memory?" Discuss some or all of the following questions.

❖ What is your earliest Christmas memory? How, if at all, does it shape your experience of Christmas now?

❖ Luke carefully remembers and reports many circumstances surrounding Jesus' birth. Read the following about Luke's remembering, then answer this question: *What is one thing you will do to make this Christmas worth remembering?*

— Luke remembers the political situation into which Jesus was born (**2:1-2**). How does remembering that "the Lord" (**2:11**) was born during the reign of a Roman emperor who commanded the obedience of "all the world" (**2:1**, NRSV) shape the way Christians relate to those in authority over us?

— Luke remembers that Jesus' adoptive father, Joseph, "belonged to David's house and family line" (**2:4**). How does remembering that the Messiah was Jewish and could claim descent from David, Israel's greatest king, shape the way Christians relate to Jewish people today?

— Luke remembers that Mary and Joseph were essentially homeless during the registration that brought them to Bethlehem (**2:7**) and that news of Jesus' birth came first to poor shepherds (**2:8**). How does remembering that Jesus was born among people who were poor and lived on society's margins shape the way Christians relate to such people today?

Responding to God's Word

Leader: *Choose one or more of the following activities.*

Play a Memory Game

Play a fun game that reminds us how Mary remembered and "turned over" the shepherds' news. On 24 index cards write out **Luke 2:11** (CEB), one word per card, until you've written the full verse twice: "Your savior is born today in David's city. He is Christ the Lord." Shuffle the cards and arrange them facedown in four rows of six. Take turns turning over two cards at a time. If you turn over matching words, remove the cards and take another turn; if not, put the cards back in their places and move to the next player. The player who makes the most matches wins—if he or she can recite the verse from memory! If not, the chance to win passes to the player with the second most matches, and so on, until a winner is found!

> **Leader:** *You will need 24 index cards, and a marker.*

Examine a Christmas Memory

Practice the contemplative remembering that Mary models with the following prayer pattern, inspired by the examen prayer of Ignatius Loyola (the sixteenth-century Spanish priest who founded the Jesuit order of priests). Sitting comfortably, pray for the Holy Spirit's guidance as you recall a Christmas memory. Don't feel rushed. When a strong memory occurs to you, review it in as much detail as you can. "Replay" it like a mental movie. (Some people find keeping a journal of their prayer examinations helpful.) Now ask:

> **Leader:** *Paper and pens or pencils for journaling are optional.*

- ❖ What, if anything, about this memory makes me aware of God's presence and love?
- ❖ What, if anything, about this memory makes me aware of my need for God's forgiveness?

❖ Who was with me at the time? How might God have been meeting me through them? How might God have been meeting them through me?
❖ Why might the Spirit have led me to this memory at this time?
❖ What is God calling me to do today through this memory?

Do Something Unforgettable!

If you have Internet access, check out the "Christmas Food Court Flash Mob" at *http://youtu.be/SXh7JR9oKVE*. That's one Christmas memory those shoppers likely will have for a long

Leader: You will need Internet access.

time! Your group may not be able to organize an operatic flash mob, but you can find or make a memorable Christmas opportunity of your own. Do some impromptu caroling in your church's neighborhood; volunteer as a group at a local soup kitchen or homeless shelter; staff a gift-wrap station at a mall or shopping center (with appropriate permissions). Whatever your group decides, do something that will bring you into contact with others and will provide an opportunity to give your time and energy as an expression of Jesus' love.

Daily Devotions

This week think and pray about how Jesus' mother Mary is an example for Christians today. What can we learn from her about living as faithful followers of her son, Jesus Christ?

MONDAY: Luke 1:26-38

From the first time we meet her, Mary is thoughtful: She puzzles through the angel Gabriel's unexpected greeting (**1:29**). When have you felt perplexed by God? How did you respond? What did it take, or what would it take, for you to trust God, even when confused, as Mary trusted God (**1:38**)?

TUESDAY: Luke 1:46-55

The song of praise Mary offers to God is known in Christian tradition as the Magnificat (from the Latin for its first words, "My soul magnifies"). Notice how Mary, remembering God's ancient promises to Israel, believes that her baby's birth signals the birth of a brand new world. How easy or hard would it be for you to "magnify" or praise God, as she does, for turning society as we know it upside down, and why?

WEDNESDAY: Luke 2:25-35

How do you imagine Mary reacted to Simeon's prophecy concerning not only her son but also this "sword" in her "innermost being" (**2:35**)? Simeon may be saying that Mary will feel pain when she sees Jesus being rejected (**2:34**), or that the conflict Jesus' work as Savior causes will touch her own family (see **Mark 3:20-21, 31-35**). What emotional risks are you willing to take to follow Jesus?

THURSDAY: *Luke* 2:41-52

Mary took her adolescent son's response to her worry in remarkably good stride (**2:51**)! When have you, as she did, "cherished every word" a child has said to you (perhaps a younger sibling, or a child in your congregation)? How have you seen little kids leading others, including yourself, to a greater awareness of God?

FRIDAY: *John* 2:1-12

She's not named here, but in this story Mary offers one of the Bible's most on-point summaries of what it means to follow her son: "Do whatever he tells you" (**2:5**). Try using her words as a breath prayer: As you breathe in, say or think, "Lord Jesus Christ"; as you breathe out, say or think, "Let me do whatever you tell me." What is Jesus telling you to do this Christmas?

SATURDAY: *Acts* 1:12-14

Jesus formed a new family, one that reached beyond biological bonds, but included his mother Mary and his brothers. As you prepare to worship tomorrow at church, think about and give thanks for your parents and siblings in Christian faith. What memories of time spent with them make you more aware of God?

WEEK FIVE

The Word

John 1:1-5

In the beginning was the Word
and the Word was with God
and the Word was God.
The Word was with God in the beginning.
Everything came into being through the Word,
and without the Word nothing came into being.
What came into being
through the Word was life,
and the life was the light for all people.
The light shines in the darkness,
and the darkness doesn't extinguish the light.

Seeing Stars

Have you seen any hot, young stars lately?

No, I don't mean have you spotted any attractive teen celebrities. I mean actual hot, young stars: newly formed, flaming balls of gas in deep space, just hatched from the swirling, cosmic clouds of a nebula. The only way you can answer "yes" to that question is if you've been paying attention to the astounding images that come back from the high-tech observation tools scientists have launched into space. The stars we can see with our unaided eye are old ones—really old, on the order of hundreds of millions of years. They can be pretty impressive, of course, but if you really want to see hot, young stars, you'll need more perceptive power than your eyes can provide on their own.

You'll need something like the Herschel Space Observatory. It can see the light spectrum from the far infrared to the sub-millimeter. Or enlist the aid of XMM-Newton, a telescope with some of the most powerful mirrors ever made and cameras that can see more X-rays than any others. When you focus these fabulous devices on the far reaches of space, you can essentially look back in time to see stars taking shape (how awesome is that?!). Check out some of NASA's snapshots of the Eagle Nebula, for instance, and you'll see brand-spanking new, super-hot stars mixing it up with gas and dust that's only a few degrees above absolute zero (that's -459.67 degrees Fahrenheit, or -273.15 Celsius; if you think you've been cold this winter, absolute zero puts things in perspective!). The atmosphere blocks the far infrared and X-ray wavelengths from earthbound observers. Without the help of our proxy peepers in the heavens, we'd never be able to witness these stars being born. We'd never see these lights shining in darkness.

The Eagle-Eyed Evangelist

John the Evangelist (a word that, in this case, means "author of a gospel") is the biblical equivalent of Herschel and XMM-Newton. In Christian art, John often is symbolized by an eagle. Soaring at great heights, eagles can still see their prey on the ground. Similarly, John possesses an exceptionally sharp theological vision, and with it he "flies high," especially in the first eighteen verses of his Gospel. Commonly called the Prologue to John's Gospel, these verses allow us to see Christ with a fantastic focus and on a cosmic scale we simply couldn't achieve on our own.

The oldest thing astronomers have seen in the sky (as of this writing—space scientists seem to be breaking such records with increasing frequency) is a galaxy more than 13 billion light-years away, meaning that it omitted the light we're seeing now 13 billion years ago. As far back in time as that observation reaches, however, John peers back even further, back to the very beginning. Echoing the first verses of the Bible's first book, John looks back to the origin of all time and space and sees God. John writes of the Word, the Word who "was with God" and who "was God" (**1:1**). The Word is that divine force of creativity that brings order out of chaos; as we read repeatedly in Genesis 1, "God said . . . And there was." John sees that everything owes its existence to the Word. The Word is why there is something rather than nothing. The Word is why there is order in the universe and not just infinite chaos. The Word is the ultimate source of all life and of all light.

What John also sees, with laser-like clarity, is that the Word is none other than Jesus of Nazareth. "The Word became flesh," writes John, "and made his home among us. We have seen his glory" (**1:14**). Don't rush over that verse. Sit with that for a minute. Don't let the fact that John's Gospel doesn't start by telling about shepherds or angels or Mary and Joseph fool you into thinking that he doesn't tell a Christmas story. This is it, and it's amazing!

John is making an audacious, breathtaking, mind-blowing claim. According to John, when you're dealing with Jesus, you're dealing with the One who created everything that was, is, or ever will be, and who still holds everything together. In Jesus, says John, the Creator became a creature; the Maker became mortal. The light of life no longer merely shone *on* the world; in Jesus, that light shone *in* the world (**1:9**).

With his eagle-eyed view of Jesus' identity, John provides a perspective we could never achieve on our own. Were John to choose a favorite Christmas song, he might select "Do You See What I See?"—not so much for its actual content (that sentimental stuff about the night wind talking to the little lamb)—as for its wonderful title. In his Prologue, John asks us, expectantly, "Do you see what I see?" Not everyone did then, and not everyone does now. But those who do—those who see and welcome Jesus the Light—become the children of God (see **John 1:10-13**).

Keep the Light in Sight!

Depending on how the calendar has worked out during the year you read these words, another Christmas Day is here or has just barely passed. The gifts have been opened (and hopefully their novelty hasn't yet worn off), the turkey has been carved (and you may be eating the leftovers for a while), and the visiting relatives have returned home (or soon will; we'll let you keep your feelings about that to yourself). That 24-7 Christmas music radio station? It's switched back to regular programming. The ornaments in your nearest gift shop? They're being priced for clearance. All those TV commercials starring Santa? Gone from the airwaves without a trace. The signs are all around and unmistakable: Another Christmas is fading fast.

Now, maybe you're ready to move on, but I'm guessing a lot of you aren't. The back half of the holiday season isn't much fun. Sure, there may still be some New Year's plans to anticipate, but not long after the crystal ball has dropped and the fireworks have exploded, it's back to school and to whatever forms of everyday bedlam your life involves.

A twentieth-century British poet named W.H. Auden wrote the saddest lines of Christmas poetry I know. Reflecting on the end of yet another holiday season, the narrator of the poem says, "Once again as in previous years we have seen the actual Vision and failed to do more than entertain it as an agreeable possibility."[1] How tragic! My hope and prayer for us, as another New Year arrives, is that we will do far more than treat the Vision we've seen this Advent and Christmas as an "agreeable possibility." I hope and pray that we, with John the Evangelist, will keep our eyes fixed on Jesus the Light.

So, practically speaking, how can we keep the Light in sight? We don't need fancy orbital telescopes, but we do need spiritual disciplines such as the following:

❖ **Pray.** Every day. More than once a day! Some people like to follow a formal pattern of prayer; others offer short, spontaneous prayers throughout the day. Pray silently or aloud. Write your prayers in a journal. Doodle them in a sketchbook. Sing them. Whatever you do, keep communicating with Christ. He is always with us; we need only grow in our awareness of his nearness.

❖ **Read Scripture.** I know it might sound like a homework assignment. And if you haven't been regularly reading the Bible, it might even feel like one—for a bit. But the more you read your Bible, the more you will be amazed at how God breathes new life into these ancient words, using them to speak to you and give you light for your path through life.

❖ **Spend time with other Christians.** There's no such thing as an independent Christian. Not only are we dependent on Christ but also we're connected to one another. We need one another for mutual support and encouragement as we strive to keep looking at the Light, because the darkness in our world and in our lives can seem so overpowering. In worshiping and studying and serving together, we can see God at work in one another's lives.

❖ **Give.** Give your time, your energy, your money, and whatever else you can think of to those who need it. And give it all from your heart. When you give to others in Jesus' name, you're not only seeing his light—you're reflecting and spreading it.

May God grant us growth in our ability to keep "the actual Vision" in front of us as we face the year ahead, and all the years to come.

May God show us, more and more, that the light shines in the darkness, and the darkness cannot overcome it (see **John 1:5**).

And may God make us unafraid to engage the bedlam of our lives—for, after all, as the angels shouted to the shepherds: To us, in bedlam, is born a Savior!

[1] From *FOR THE TIME BEING: A Christmas Oratorio,* by W.H. Auden (London: Faber and Faber, 1955); p. 123.

Light the Advent Candles

Recruit several youth to read aloud the following litany, with the entire group responding by saying the boldfaced text.

Leader: You will need an Advent wreath, five wax or electric candles, and hymnals or songbooks including "Hark! the Herald Angels Sing."

The Lord be with you!
And also with you!

"Your loyal love, LORD,
    extends to the skies;
    your faithfulness reaches the clouds . . .
Within you is the spring of life.
    In your light, we see light" (**Psalm 36:5, 9**).

In Jesus Christ, God comes down and shines in the midst of our darkness!

"God said that light should shine out of the darkness. He is the same one who shone in our hearts to give us the light of the knowledge of God's glory in the face of Jesus Christ" (**2 Corinthians 4:6**).

Light all four Advent candles, and the fifth, Christmas candle.

Glorious God, you live in unapproachable light;
    but out of love you shine your saving grace on us and on the world in
        your Word made flesh, Jesus Christ.
For his sake, send your Spirit to keep our sight focused on him,
    so we may shine like stars in the world,
    reflecting your love's light to all around us.

Read or sing together "Hark! the Herald Angels Sing" (Stanza 4);
The United Methodist Hymnal, *240.*

Hail the heaven-born Prince of Peace!
Hail the Sun of Righteousness!

Light and life to all he brings, risen with healing in his wings.
Mild he lays his glory by, born that we no more may die,
  born to raise us from the earth, born to give us second birth.
Hark! the herald angels sing, "Glory to the newborn King!"
—WORDS: Charles Wesley (1734)

Unto us is born in bedlam a Savior!
Thanks be to God!

Exchange words and gestures of peace with one another.

Hear God's Word

Read John 1:1-5, then the article for Week Five, "Seeing Stars." Discuss some or all of the following questions.

- ❖ What do you associate with light? What makes light such a powerful symbol of God's presence and activity?
- ❖ Where and how do you see evidence of the light of Christ shining in darkness today?
- ❖ Which spiritual discipline(s) discussed in this week's article (see page 53) help you best keep Jesus' light in sight? What other disciplines or practices would you suggest?

Responding to God's Word

Leader: Choose one or more of the following activities.

Pray With an Icon

In the Eastern Orthodox Christian tradition, believers often pray using icons. Icons aren't intended to be realistic portraits of their subjects, which frequently are the people and events of Scripture; rather, they are painted (or "written") to be "windows" through which we "gaze" into the light of God. As one author, Father Stephen Bonian, explains, "The primary power of icons lies in their physicality: they make the presence of the holy tangible. They rouse the imagination and generate emotions in the viewer."[2] While some Christians wrongly equate icons with idols, Orthodox Christians believe that icons honor the Incarnation of God's Word—the truth that, in Jesus of Nazareth, God had a human face. Father Bonian explains: "God chose to become matter so that we can see, touch and be present with him through our material world,"[3] and praying with icons is one way of doing so.

Find an icon of Jesus, perhaps one that depicts his birth, or an icon known as "Christ the Light-Giver." (Google to the rescue!) Spend some time praying in the presence of the icon. Sit comfortably, gazing steadily at the icon. Notice any details to which your eyes are drawn: What might they symbolize? Notice also any thoughts or feelings the icon prompts in you. How might God be using these reactions to speak with you?

There are no hard and fast, "right and wrong" rules for praying with icons. As with last week's memory examination, you might find recording your reactions to be helpful. Icons are a means, not an end, to heartfelt communication with God.

Scheduling Scripture Reading

According to *The Encyclopedia of Superstitions*, "In order to find out whether the coming year would be fortunate or otherwise, the inquirer opened the Bible at random on New Year's morning . . . and without looking at the page, thrust a pin into it, or laid his finger upon it. The verse thus blindly chosen foretold the good or evil nature of the following twelve months."[4]

We don't recommend such a random way of choosing the Bible verses you'll read each day! Instead, make a plan and try to stick to it as much as possible. You may not want to commit to a "through the Bible in a year" reading plan, and that's OK; instead, you might like to read one psalm a day, or work your way through, chapter at a time, a biblical book that's always seemed interesting to you.

You might also want to check out daily readings and related prayers available through such websites and mobile apps as The Daily Office West (*www.dailyoffice.org*) or Daily Prayer PC(USA) (available through iTunes). When you follow these calendars, you know you're reading the same Scriptures as thousands of other Christians on the same day, and that knowledge can encourage you as you follow the discipline of regular Bible reading.

Wesley on Wealth

John Wesley, the founder of Methodism, famously exhorted his followers to:

◈ **Gain all you can**—to use your God-given gifts and abilities to avoid idleness and earn a productive living;
◈ **Save all you can**—not an invitation to hoard money, but to use it frugally, cutting expenses and cutting out indulgences wherever possible;
◈ **Give all you can**—to those who have so little. "If the Methodists would give all they can," Wesley remarked, "then all would have enough."

Draw three columns on a sheet of paper and label one each as "GAIN," "SAVE," and "GIVE." In each column, list specific ways you could gain more, save more, and give more in the coming year. Share your responses with another Christian whom you trust to hold you accountable. As next year's Christmas season approaches, review your responses and evaluate how well you met the challenge of this spiritual discipline. Give thanks for your successes; pray for God's pardon and power where you could have done better; and begin the process again. Trust the Spirit to transform you through the discipline of giving!

[2] Stephen Bonian, S.J., "Gateways to Prayer," *America*, December 8, 2008, para 3, *http://americamagazine.org/issue/679/article/gateways-prayer*
[3] From "Gateways to Prayer," last paragraph.
[4] From *The Encyclopedia of Superstitions,* edited by Christina Hole (New York: Barnes & Noble Books, 1948, 1961; 1996); page 46.

Daily Devotions

This week think and pray about some other images for Jesus we find in John's Gospel. Light is not the only one. How can these images help us keep our sight fixed on Jesus?

MONDAY: John 1:43-51

Jesus' seemingly strange words to Nathanael may make more sense when we realize Jesus is comparing himself ("the Son of Man") to a heavenly vision seen by the patriarch Jacob in a dream (see **Genesis 28:10-17** for details). How might Jesus be like the ladder Jacob saw connecting heaven to earth?

TUESDAY: John 6:25-35, 51

Another story from Hebrew Scripture in which Jesus found an image for himself was the story of God feeding the freed Israelite slaves during their wilderness wanderings (see **Exodus 16**). How is Jesus both like and unlike the manna that came down from heaven? How does Jesus feed us?

WEDNESDAY: John 10:1-15

Jesus uses two images for himself drawn from the everyday experience of shepherds. One is a personal image (shepherd); the other isn't (gate). In what sense is Jesus like a gate or door? How is it possible to enter through him—and to what or where? And how is Jesus a good shepherd? What do you do to listen for his voice as he leads you?

THURSDAY: John 11:17-27

Many (but not all) first-century Jews believed that, in the last days of history, God would raise dead people to everlasting life (see, for example, **Daniel 12:2-3**). What does Jesus mean, then, when he tells Martha that he, himself, is this resurrection? How do you experience eternal life through Jesus right now?

FRIDAY: John 14:1-7

What claim does Jesus make with these words? How and why was Jesus reassuring his followers by making this statement?

SATURDAY: John 15:1-11

If possible, spend some time observing a fruit growing on a vine. How is Jesus like a vine? How does he say we can abide or remain in him? When have you felt "fruitful" in your life as a Christian? When have you felt "fruitless"? What task will you face with greater confidence and joy knowing that you are abiding in Jesus?

Bonus:

Organize a Churchwide Advent Study

Finding Bethlehem in the Midst of Bedlam helps Christians focus on the good news of Jesus' birth during what is, for many, the most chaotic time of the year. Finding Bethlehem offers Advent study resources for youth, adults, and children, and allows for the possibility of a churchwide, intergenerational program.

Such a program gives youth, adults, and children opportunities to learn from one another, to worship together, and to work together to serve the community in a spirit of Christ's love. Families can be intentional about setting aside this time each week for learning, fellowship, devotion, and a welcome break from seasonal bedlam.

Resources for the Churwide Study

Adults: *Finding Bethlehem in the Midst of Bedlam* by James W. Moore (9781426760822)

Youth: *Finding Bethlehem in the Midst of Bedlam—An Advent Study for Youth* by Mike Poteet (9781426768996)

Children: *Finding Bethlehem in the Midst of Bedlam—An Advent Study for Children* by Brittany Sky (9781426769016)

Schedule Suggestions

Many churches have weeknight programs that include an evening meal, an intergenerational gathering time, and classes for children, youth, and adults. The following schedule illustrates one way to organize a weeknight program.

❖ **5:30 P.M.:** Gather for a meal.
❖ **6:00 P.M.:** Lead an intergenerational gathering that introduces the subject and primary Scriptures for that evening's session. This time may include presentations, skits, music, and opening or closing prayers.
❖ **6:15 P.M.–8:45 P.M.:** Gather in classes for children, youth, and adults.

You may choose to position this study as a Sunday school program. This approach would be similar to the weeknight schedule, except with a shorter class time (which is common for Sunday morning programs).

❖ **10 minutes:** Lead an intergenerational gathering that is similar to the one described above.
❖ **45 minutes:** Gather in classes for children, youth, and adults.

Choose a schedule that works best for your congregation and its existing Christian education programs.

Activity Suggestions

Provide a Respite From the Bedlam

Find a way to serve the many people in your community who are also in need of a break from the bedlam. Consider offering a free gift-wrapping service or set up a table in a high-traffic shopping area and provide free coffee and/or hot chocolate.

Your simple gesture will give people a glimpse of God's love and possibly a moment of peace during the chaos of holiday preparations and seasonal obligations.

House of Bread

The Week One session points out that the name *Bethlehem* means "house of bread" in Hebrew and suggests baking Christmas cookies or bread as a reminder that Jesus, the "bread of life," was born in the "house of bread."

Instead of just baking bread or cookies as a part of the youth study, consider making it an intergenerational activity. If you gather for a meal, arrange each week for certain families to provide baked goods for dessert. Between the meal and dessert read aloud John 6:35. ("Jesus replied, 'I am the bread of life. Whoever comes to me will never go hungry, and whoever believes in me will never be thirsty.' ") Then say a prayer of thanks for the nourishment that Jesus provides.

Another option would be to hold a baked goods auction with all proceeds going to a ministry or mission organization that seeks to provide relief to people who experience bedlam (whether in the form of hunger, addiction, homelessness, or something else).

Sympathy With the Imprisoned

The "Sympathy With the Imprisoned" activity (page 24) from Week Two is another churchwide possibility. It suggests arranging a gift collection for the children of inmates through a ministry such as Prison Fellowship's Angel Tree.

Prison Fellowship's Angel Tree

Expand this activity (page 24) by having each age group, class, or family commit to purchasing gifts for one child. Lead a time of blessing for the gifts during your gathering time.

Impromptu Interview

If your group does the "Impromptu Interview" activity (page 34) from Week Three, show the finished video to the entire congregation during the following week's churchwide gathering.

❖ ❖ ❖ ❖ **Notes** ❖ ❖ ❖ ❖